MICROSOFT ONENOTE QUICK START 2024 GUIDE

JEXONIA GRANEER

Copyright © 2023 Jexonia Graneer
All rights reserved.

INTRODUCTION

Context Setting

In the digital age, the art of note-taking and information management has evolved dramatically. Gone are the days of pen and paper being the sole tools for jotting down ideas and organizing thoughts. In a world where the speed of information exchange and the volume of data we handle daily continue to grow, the need for efficient, versatile, and reliable digital tools has never been greater.

Introducing Microsoft OneNote

Enter Microsoft OneNote, a cutting-edge digital notebook that has transformed the way we capture, store, and share information. Since its inception, OneNote has stood out as a comprehensive solution for individuals and organizations seeking to streamline their note-taking and collaborative endeavors. As we approach 2024, this guide delves into the latest iteration of OneNote, showcasing its robust features and the innovative ways it continues to redefine digital organization.

Key Features and Enhancements in the 2024 Edition

The 2024 edition of Microsoft OneNote brings a plethora of enhancements and new features, building upon its already impressive capabilities. This edition has been meticulously engineered to offer a more intuitive user experience, enhanced integration with other Microsoft products, and superior cloud connectivity. Whether you are a seasoned OneNote user or new to the platform, this guide will walk you through these advancements, ensuring you can leverage the full potential of OneNote.

Navigating the Interface

At the heart of Microsoft OneNote's appeal is its user-friendly interface. The layout is designed with the user in mind, offering an intuitive, easy-to-navigate experience that belies its comprehensive functionality. From the get-go, this guide will introduce you to the fundamental aspects of the OneNote interface, providing you with the confidence to start organizing your digital life immediately.

Organizational Capabilities

One of OneNote's core strengths lies in its unparalleled organizational capabilities. Whether you're managing complex projects, categorizing research notes, or simply keeping your daily tasks in order, OneNote offers a flexible and customizable environment to suit your needs. This guide will explore these capabilities in depth, demonstrating how OneNote can be your ultimate ally in digital organization.

Delving further into OneNote's organizational prowess, it's important to understand how it transcends the traditional boundaries of note-taking. The 2024 edition introduces enhanced tagging and searching features, making the retrieval of information as effortless as possible. Imagine a digital workspace where every note, every piece of data, is just a few clicks away, regardless of the volume. This section of the introduction would explore these features in depth, providing real-life scenarios where such capabilities could be transformative.

Moreover, the customizability of OneNote sets it apart. Users are not just confined to a rigid structure of note organization; instead, they can tailor their digital notebooks to mirror their thought processes and work habits. This guide will walk you through creating a personalized digital notebook, from setting up basic structures to implementing advanced organizational techniques.

Collaboration and Sharing

In today's interconnected world, the ability to collaborate and share information seamlessly is paramount. OneNote excels in this area, offering a range of features designed to facilitate cooperation, whether in a professional setting, within educational environments, or for personal projects. We will delve into these collaborative tools, illustrating how OneNote can transform your teamwork and information-sharing workflows.

Collaboration in OneNote is not just about sharing notes; it's about creating a dynamic workspace where teams can interact, edit, and brainstorm in real-time. The 2024 edition brings improvements in synchronization speed and reliability, ensuring that team members are always on the same page, literally and figuratively.

We will delve into the nuances of shared notebooks, discussing permissions, real-time editing, and even the integration of collaborative tools like Microsoft Teams. This section aims to demonstrate how OneNote can be the central hub for team projects, where ideas converge and evolve into tangible outcomes.

Additionally, we'll explore the role of OneNote in remote work and learning environments, a reality that has become increasingly prominent. How does OneNote facilitate a seamless transition between office, home, and classroom settings? This guide will provide insights and tips on making the most of OneNote in various collaborative contexts.

Advanced Customization and Integration

Beyond basic note-taking and organization, OneNote offers a range of advanced customization options and integrations. In this part of the introduction, we delve into the possibilities unlocked by these features. This includes everything from integrating OneNote with other Microsoft 365 applications to using add-ins and APIs for specialized tasks.

For instance, the integration with Outlook for task management or with Excel for data import and analysis reveals the multifaceted nature of OneNote. We will provide practical examples and step-by-step guides on leveraging these integrations to enhance your productivity and streamline your workflows.

Security and Accessibility

In today's digital age, security and accessibility are crucial. This section of the introduction will cover the robust security features of OneNote, ensuring that your data remains protected in a world where cybersecurity threats are ever-present. We'll discuss encryption, password protection, and secure sharing options.

Accessibility is another key focus. OneNote's design adheres to Microsoft's commitment to inclusivity, offering features like Immersive Reader and accessibility checking tools. This guide will highlight how these features make OneNote an effective tool for users with diverse needs and preferences.

Setting the Stage for Mastery

As we round off the introduction, we set the stage for what is to come in the subsequent chapters. This guide is not just about understanding OneNote; it's about mastering it. Whether you're a first-time user or looking to deepen your existing knowledge, the chapters that follow will provide a comprehensive journey through all that OneNote has to offer.

From managing personal projects to collaborating in a corporate environment, from basic note-taking to advanced data organization, this guide will equip you with the knowledge and skills to make OneNote an integral part of your digital toolkit.

CONTENTS

INTRODUCTION

CONTENTS

Chapter 1: introducing Microsoft ONENOTE... 1

Chapter 2: Getting Acquainted with Microsoft OneNote 9

Chapter 3: Managing and Collaborating........ 17

Chapter 4: Input and Customization Techniques 31

Chapter 5: Mastering Section Groups 35

Chapter 6: Enhancing OneNote with Add-ins 39

Chapter 7: OneNote for Effective Project Management 47

Chapter 8: Evaluating OneNote's Effectiveness 55

Chapter 9: Keyboard shortcuts in OneNote .. 63

Conclusion 71

CHAPTER 1: INTRODUCING MICROSOFT ONENOTE

Introduction to Microsoft OneNote

Microsoft OneNote 2024 stands as a pivotal element in the suite of productivity tools provided by Microsoft. It's an advanced digital notebook that offers unparalleled flexibility and integration, allowing users to gather, organize, and share notes and information in a dynamic, user-friendly interface.

What is Microsoft OneNote?

At its core, Microsoft OneNote is a digital note-taking application that provides a single place for all your notes, ideas, lists, and reminders. It's the quintessence of digital organization, offering a canvas where text, images, audio, and video can be placed freely—mimicking the non-linear way in which our brains process information. OneNote is designed to function like a physical notebook, but with the added benefits of digital technology, such as searching for text, tagging, and even handwriting recognition.

The Digital Notebook Revolution

OneNote has spearheaded the digital notebook revolution, moving us away from the era of scattered sticky notes and disjointed documents. With features that support collaboration, OneNote enables multiple users to work on the same page simultaneously, thus revolutionizing group projects and remote work. Its ability to sync across devices ensures that your information follows you wherever you go.

Understanding OneNote

OneNote has woven itself into the fabric of everyday tasks and professional workflows, owing to its adaptability and ease of use.

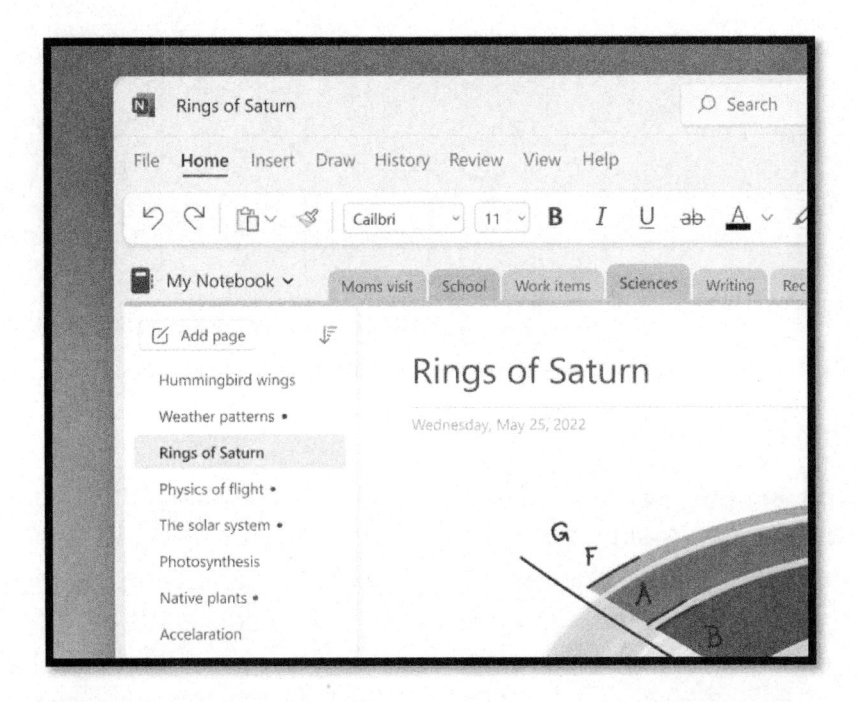

OneNote in Everyday Life

For everyday use, OneNote acts as the ultimate repository. Whether it's meal planning, tracking fitness routines, or maintaining a personal journal, OneNote accommodates a variety of templates and organizational structures that cater to the individual needs of its users. Its intuitive design allows users to capture thoughts and tasks with minimal disruption to their daily flow.

OneNote for Students and Professionals

In the realm of education and professionalism, OneNote functions as an extension of one's cognitive processes. Students utilize it for taking lecture notes, organizing research, and group studying. For professionals, it serves as a dashboard for project management, meeting minutes, and strategic planning. The integration with Microsoft's suite of tools, like Outlook for task management and SharePoint for document storage, further cements OneNote's position as a cornerstone of professional productivity.

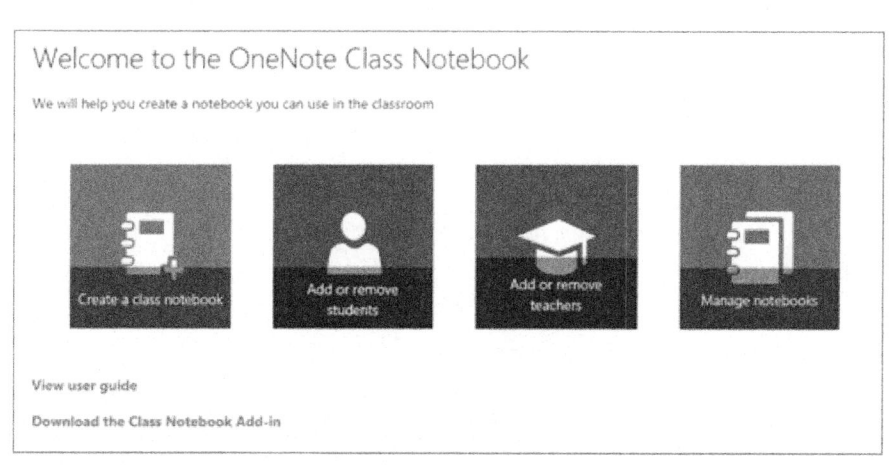

OneNote Across Devices

The accessibility of OneNote is a hallmark of its design philosophy. Whether on a laptop, tablet, or smartphone, OneNote's interface provides a seamless experience. This cross-device compatibility ensures that the information is accessible and editable on any device, allowing users to continue working on their notes regardless of their physical location or the device in hand.

The Development History of OneNote

The evolution of OneNote reflects Microsoft's commitment to innovation and responsiveness to user feedback.

The Early Days of Digital Note-Taking

OneNote's inception was a response to the growing need for a digital solution that could replicate the versatility and simplicity of paper notebooks. Early versions focused on basic note organization, providing a freeform canvas and the ability to create multiple sections and pages.

OneNote's Evolution Over the Years

Over the years, OneNote has undergone significant transformations. Microsoft diligently added features like shared notebooks, handwriting recognition, and deep integration with Office tools. Cloud synchronization came into play, enabling real-time updates and collaboration.

What's New in OneNote 2024?

The 2024 version of OneNote boasts an array of new features and enhancements. It delivers a more streamlined user experience, with a refined interface that reduces clutter and focuses on note-taking. Advanced AI features are a game-changer, offering contextual suggestions, summarization capabilities, and enhanced search functionality that can predict and locate information instantaneously.

In conclusion, Microsoft OneNote 2024 is not merely an update but a reimagining of the digital note-taking landscape. It is designed for the modern user who juggles multiple roles and demands efficiency and connectivity. As we delve further into the specifics in the following sections, we will uncover how OneNote can be tailored to fit personal and professional environments, demonstrating its versatility and power as a tool for organization, collaboration, and productivity.

Getting OneNote

Embarking on the journey of digital note-taking with Microsoft OneNote 2024 begins with obtaining the software. Microsoft offers several avenues for acquiring OneNote, catering to various user needs and preferences.

Subscription Options

Microsoft OneNote 2024 is accessible through several subscription models, primarily under the umbrella of Microsoft 365, the company's comprehensive service that bundles together various applications and services.

Microsoft 365 Personal: Ideal for individual users, this subscription provides access to OneNote along with other Office applications such as Word, Excel, and PowerPoint, plus additional OneDrive storage and Skype minutes for calls.

Microsoft 365 Family: Designed for households, this plan extends all the benefits of the Personal subscription to up to six users, each with their unique OneDrive storage.

Microsoft 365 Business: Tailored for organizations, the business plans range from basic to premium offerings, incorporating OneNote as part of a package that includes business email, teamwork and communication tools, and advanced security options.

Each subscription comes with the added benefit of regular updates, ensuring that users always have the latest features and security enhancements.

OneNote Standalone Purchase

For users who prefer a one-time purchase without the commitment to a subscription, Microsoft offers OneNote as part of the Office Home & Student package. This option includes a standalone version of OneNote along with other essential Office apps, allowing for use on a single computer.

Price Considerations

When choosing how to acquire OneNote, considering the pricing models is crucial for making an informed decision that aligns with both budget and usage requirements.

OneNote Pricing Models

The subscription-based model, Microsoft 365, operates on a yearly or monthly payment plan. It offers the advantage of continuously receiving the latest updates and features without additional costs. The standalone version, while lacking the subscription benefits, requires only a single upfront payment and can be an economical choice for users with static needs.

Finding the Best Deal for Your Needs

To find the best deal, evaluate how you plan to use OneNote. For example, students and educators may be eligible for discounts or even free access through their institutions.

Businesses might benefit from volume licensing or bundle offers that combine several Microsoft services at a reduced cost. Comparing the total value of bundled applications and services against individual needs can help in choosing the most cost-effective option.

Installing Microsoft OneNote

Once the purchase or subscription is settled, installing OneNote is the next step.

System Requirements for OneNote 2024

Before installation, ensure your device meets the minimum system requirements for OneNote 2024, which typically include:

- A modern operating system (the latest version of Windows, macOS, iOS, or Android)
- Sufficient RAM and processor speed for smooth operation
- Adequate hard disk space for installation and data storage
- An active internet connection for installation, updates, and synchronization of notes

Step-by-Step Installation Guide

Installation steps for OneNote will vary slightly depending on the device and the source of your software (Microsoft 365 subscription or standalone Office package).

For Microsoft 365 Subscribers:

- Visit the Microsoft 365 portal and sign in with your Microsoft account.
- Navigate to the 'Install Office' section on the home page.
- Select 'Install Office' to download the installer.
- Once downloaded, run the installer and follow the on-screen instructions to complete the setup.

For Standalone Office Users:

- After purchasing Office Home & Student, you'll receive a product key.
- Visit the setup page indicated by the retailer or in your confirmation email and enter your product key.
- Sign in with your Microsoft account, or create one if you don't have it.
- Download the installer, run it, and follow the prompts to install the Office apps, including OneNote.

Troubleshooting Installation Issues

Installation issues can arise due to outdated software, lack of storage, or interrupted internet connections. Common troubleshooting steps include:

- Restarting your device and attempting the installation again.
- Checking for updates on your operating system and ensuring all critical updates are installed.
- Clearing space on your device if storage is insufficient.
- Using a wired connection if Wi-Fi is unstable.

If you encounter specific error codes, Microsoft's support website provides detailed guides and community forums for resolving such issues.

In conclusion, acquiring and setting up Microsoft OneNote 2024 is a straightforward process designed to accommodate users from various walks of life. Whether opting for a subscription service or a standalone purchase, OneNote is accessible and scalable to your specific note-taking needs. With a focus on ease of installation and robust support, Microsoft ensures that beginning your journey with OneNote is as seamless as the user experience it aims to provide within the application itself.

CHAPTER 2: GETTING ACQUAINTED WITH MICROSOFT ONENOTE

In other words, this is an app that helps one who has a very busy schedule to be more organized and to ensure that all their marvelous and intriguing ideas are captured for later reference. It is very normal for human beings to forget, and we tend to forget a lot. More often than not, you get an idea, and since you did not put it down on pen and paper, you try as hard as you can to remember what the idea you had at the time was to no avail. By learning how to use OneNote, those days are as good as behind you. Read on to discover everything you need to know to start creating a paperless life with OneNote.

When it comes to OneNote, you can expect that you will capture, organize and share all of the notes that you will be placing in your notebook. Truly, this innovative software will be the help that you need.

Who Should Use OneNote?

OneNote is most welcomed by the majority of people who hate paper trails. Having a desk full of piles and piles of papers is just unsightly and can also mess with your morale to work considering you have to go through the papers. With, OneNote, one need not worry about that mess as the app is more organized giving you a clear head and leaving you refreshed as you decide on where to start. When your mind is clear, your work becomes a tad easier, and this is why you should learn how to use the OneNote.

Why Use OneNote

When you go shopping for an application, you have in mind what you want the app to help you do. However, in most cases, you will come across numerous apps that can perform the simpler functions that you need to be done. With the wide variety of note taking applications available in the market today, it is hard to decide which of them will meet your note taking needs best. The truth is, all the apps out there can help you take notes the ordinary way. However, there is much more to taking notes than just typing what you want to capture, and saving it in your device. One of the elements that make OneNote different from another note taking apps is the suite of unique features it offers that add value to the note taking process. These features are discussed in detail later in this guide but here are some of the things that OneNote app enables you to do:

Organize Lists: Notes that are taken on OneNote can be shared with other people and any changes made by other people in your circle become visible to everyone in the group. This feature decreases chances of forgetting to purchase something you need, or a last minute requirement for a project.

Create recipe lists: In case your recipe book takes a beating due to over-use, you can transfer your recipes to the OneNote. You have the option to organize them based on main food items that you use.

Locate favorite news items: You may not realize it yet, but as you browse the internet, and add content to your OneNote, the app allows you to list the content in the order of favorite items. This makes it easy to access them again so you can read them whenever you want. This feature works well for articles and recipes.

Make audio /video recordings: When using the full version of OneNote, you can record audio and video notes to attach to your notes.

Convert Images to Text: This is probably one of the best features that OneNote has to offer. It allows you to take a picture of a page in a book you love, and it will quickly be converted to text as long as that text is easy to understand. You need not transcribe it one by one.

All these capabilities and much more make OneNote a valuable and easy to use application's go through this guide, you will discover many important features of OneNote that make it the ideal application for note taking.

If you are wondering how other people use OneNote, you will be pleased to know some of them use it the same way that you want to. They basically use the application to take notes about lessons they learn in school, deliberations from a work meeting and capture reminders of things they do not want to forget. There are people who use Microsoft OneNote to improve their lives in a significant way.

The school wants to be able to show video clips and enable students to listen to audio clips without duplication. Finding software that was capable of doing that became an easy task the moment the school tried out Microsoft 365equipped with OneNote. This software makes organizing, sharing and note taking easier.

The school started by testing the effectiveness of Microsoft 365 in various groups and departments. Initial results of these tests were favorable, with most members of the group showcasing their creativity. As time passed by, the teams started learning more about the stuff that this suite of applications allows them to do. These test outcomes informed the school's decision to use OneNote for over all note taking.

Besides the students, there are teachers who use OneNote to

connect with their class. For instance, some teachers create shared notebooks so students understand the lessons better. At the same time, the notebooks also contain necessary details on upcoming quizzes and examinations. The use of OneNote is taking note taking to degree whole new level.

How OneNote Is Organized

OneNote is organized by Notebooks, sections, and pages similar to printed, spiral-bound notebook.

Notebooks- Are the major organization category.

Sections in the current Notebook- Sections let you organize notes by activities, topic, or people in your life. You start with a few in each notebook.

Pages in the current section- Create as many note pages in each section as you want or as necessary.

After understanding how OneNote is organized, it is time for you to advance to the next level as you need to learn the basics on how to go about creating your own notebook.

The Design and Basics of OneNote

The great thing about the OneNote is its ability to look similar to the physical notebook. For users who are not quite ready to let go of their notebooks yet but at the same time would like to have the convenience of using an application, the design of this is perfect.

Expect to Have Multiple Notebooks

This is similar to having a lot of subjects in school. You cannot expect that all of the lessons that you have learned in Science will also be in the same notebook wherein you would be placing all of your notes in Math. You need to have separate notebooks so that you will know what to get.

With the OneNote, for each notebook that you have, there will be tabs that are available. As you can already guess, each tab refers to a section of the notebook that you possibly would like to pay attention to. For example, if one tab refers to your grocery list and you need to do your grocery, you can click on this and scan through it instead of having one long list of not only your grocery list but also the other things that you plan on doing.

If in case you have created new tabs but cannot find it in the multiple notebooks that you already have, simply go to Quick Notes because this is where the new notes are placed.

Share Your Notebook

In case you would like other people to have an input about the notebook that you have made, then you can simply share it with other people. After some time, you can also see their own creative input on the notes that you have placed.

Understanding Different Versions of OneNote

OneNote has a variety of versions depending on the operating system. The complete OneNote version runs on Windows.

Windows Version

If you use Windows on a touch screen enabled laptop or computer, you will be able to use OneNote in the best possible way. The application allows you to take notes with a stylus, and if you wish, you can convert them to text so that the next time you want to refer to them, they are there.

You can use inking tools to highlight text for emphasis. You may add circles or squares depending on how you think the details should be highlighted. You may also embed files that you already have in Microsoft Office to OneNote so you access this data fast whenever you need to. It is possible to embed Excel sheets, though of smaller sizes.

Without using an application such as OneNote, you might find it challenging to keep data in separate files. Your data would get all mixed up. With OneNote, you have the power to keep your items in separate files and update them on a regular basis. Though a Windows phone is designed to do all these things, installing the OneNote application enhances its ability to organize data.

iOS Version

The iOS version of OneNote comes with handwriting features that convert written notes to text. A user has the option to convert the text or leave as it is. This may then be linked to personal or business accounts. It is ideal for capturing good moments or sharing funny images with other people without mixing them up with other work related items. Previously, it was difficult to use OneNote on iOS devices due to small screens. However, this has changed in a significant way as larger iOS devices became available in the market.

Android Version

Android offers the latest version of OneNote. It is a direct competition to Google Keep, which offers seemingly similar functions. Unlike on iOS, OneNote can create different widgets that allow you to access the notes you need immediately by simply scribbling or placing a code. You can also take pictures with your phone and add them to the application. In case, you opt to be reminded of your notes, and you own an Android watch, you may choose to access such notes on your watch. This OneNote feature on Android platforms makes everything highly accessible.

Mac Version

Though the Mac version is somewhat similar to OneNote's Windows version, a few noticeable differences are observed. The Mac version allows for sharing of

notes with other people but does not allow users to add multiple accounts. This means that one has to choose whether they only want to create a personal notebook or a work notebook.

Now that you know the various OneNote versions available, you can decide which version is most helpful to you and make an informed choice. You will also find it easier to tackle problems that come your way, depending on which platform you use. Not to mention, the work is saved seamlessly and could be accessed through any device that you are already signed in.

CHAPTER 3: MANAGING AND COLLABORATING

After working on your notebook, several actions can be taken to ensure you keep track of your note. This section covers those actions which you can take to keep your notebooks secure. You can decide to share your notebook, a page, or a section with others, export or just save them.

To know more about how you can achieve these, let's go.

Sharing

If you want to share your "Personal" Notebook with anybody, you need to move it to OneDrive. To do this, open your "Personal" Notebook, navigate to "File" and then go down to your share option and what you'll see in there is it says to share this notebook, so you'll need to put it in OneDrive or SharePoint. You're going to put that in OneDrive by selecting it. You could also browse for it if you don't have it listed here, you can name your notebook and choose "Move notebook". You will get a message saying the notebook is now syncing to the new location, click on "OK". Now that you've done that you'll see that you now have all of your share options come up because you've now put it in a location where sharing is available.

Sharing with OneDrive

Finally, you have the move notebook option which you saw how to use before when you moved your notebook into OneDrive.

It's not necessary to always share the entire notebook; if you prefer you can share a single page from the notebook only. So, if you want to share a page from your notebook, make sure you've clicked on the page that you want to share, go up to the

Home tab and you'll see you have an option here to "Email page", keyboard shortcut Ctrl + Shift + E. What it does is it will open up an outlook email, it's going to attach the contents of that page, you can then select who you want to share this with and send that email off. The user receives an email that's got the name of the notebook and an open button. If they hit that it'll open up the notebook in the browser and if that user makes a change, it will sync that change and, in your notebook, you'll see the change, with a little marker indicating that it was added by the user.

Syncing And Saving

One important thing to remember when you're sharing notebooks is that there could be multiple people accessing and editing a notebook at any given time. So due to this, your notebook must be synchronized to ensure data is updated immediately.

To do this, go to the File tab and ensure you are in the "Info" area. what you'll see over on the right-hand side is you have a button here to view sync status and this is going to show all of the notebooks that you have and whether they're synchronized and the last time they were updated.

The option automatically selected is to sync automatically whenever there are changes. So, if you've shared this notebook with five other people and they're all in this notebook making changes, any changes they make are automatically synchronized so that you can see them.

However, if you prefer to sync manually you have the option as well, and as soon as you do that it puts a cross over each of these notebooks just to let you know that they're not currently synchronizing and you can choose which one you want to sync.

So, if you click "Sync Now", the icon is going to change and any updates made since the last sync will be updated. If you have a lot of notebooks in here, to make this easier you have a single button at the top as well, to "Sync All".

Password Protection

Another thing that you might want to do when sharing your notebooks is password-protect sections of the notebook. This prevents unauthorized access to specific sections of your notebook that you don't want people to see. If you want people to be able to see everything that's in one section but not in another section, all you need to do is right-click and select "Password protect This section", click "Set Password" and now if you share this notebook, people aren't going to be able to see what's on that particular section.

To unprotect, right-click, go back into "Password protect This Section", select "Remove password" and type it in to remove that protection.

Exporting Notebooks

Many of us use OneNote notebooks to organize our lives. It is important to know how to backup your OneNote because technology can fail and when it does you want to make sure your materials are safe and secure and so it is necessary to backup your work. It is highly recommended you do this at some point, especially as you get towards the end of the school year and you leave for the summer or as you're working with other members of a team. Backing up your notebook in OneNote is a great idea.

There are cases where you may not have access to OneDrive, let's say you're getting a new job, you're moving to a different district, for some unforeseeable reason your server goes down or you need access when you're not online, you need to export your OneNote. To do this, go to your "Files" tab, and instead of choosing "Save" you're going to choose "Export". You'll get several options. You can export a page, that's handy if you just want to share a page with somebody; you can share a section, or for your use, you can export your entire OneNote notebook, and you are going to have file types to choose from. You can export them as PDFs but you can't edit those in the future. To export your OneNote as a package so you can upload it into OneNote in the future as its full functioning self, you'll need to select "OneNote Package" and then you just click the export button.

You're going to tell it where to save on your device and you have your OneNote notebook saved on your hard drive for loading whatever you want, wherever you want, whether you are online or not.

This can be done for group notebooks as well, so if you're in charge of your group's notebook this is a good idea to do every once in a while, but it's also handy for individual notebooks.

How to Get started

OneNote is a free digital note-taking app from Microsoft that you can use to capture ideas and thoughts.

You can use it to create notes and add content to them and it stores your notes in the cloud. This is great if you're probably in a classroom taking notes, or if you are in a business meeting or just your for everyday life, family life, planning a vacation, and you just want to put all these ideas in one spot.

How To Get OneNote

You may be thinking of how to take advantage of OneNote and how to get to OneNote. Well, the good news is OneNote comes with Windows 10, so if you have a Windows 10 device you already have one note.

How do you get to OneNote? What you can do is you simply go down to the search field and just type in "OneNote" and what you'll see happen is OneNote will show up as the best match on the list. You can now go ahead and click on it and the OneNote app will open up. If you are a Windows 11 user, unfortunately, this application doesn't come pre-installed. For that, you just need to visit Microsoft Store and there, you can find OneNote.

Another way you could also get OneNote is from your web browser. What you could do is simply open up your web browser and then go to office.com. This is how you're going to access OneNote. Click on sign-in and if you have a Microsoft account you sign in with your Microsoft account. If you don't have a Microsoft account you could also create one for free by clicking on the create one button.

As earlier said, OneNote stores all your notes in the cloud, and because they're in the cloud it can sync those notes between all the devices you're using. So if you create a note on your phone, you'll immediately see it on your desktop. For the syncing to work you need to log into OneNote and to do this you need a Microsoft account; this could be one that you use at work or school with office 365 or from another Microsoft service like Outlook and so on.

Once you sign in you'll land on office.com and you'll see that you can access OneNote by clicking on the OneNote icon. In addition to OneNote, you could also get Word, Excel, PowerPoint, through office.com, and if you have a phone whether an Android device or an iOS device, you can also download the OneNote app from the App Store or the Google Play Store and you can install that on your phone.

Here, I'm going to show you the Windows 10 version of the OneNote app but the look and feel are pretty similar across all the different platforms it's supported on.

The Hierarchy

A great feature in OneNote is that you can create your hierarchy structure. There are three main levels, the highest level Is the Notebook, and just like the physical notebook, they can hold many pages. The next level down is Sections. Think of this like chapters in a book. And finally, there are Pages. These hold your actual notes.

If you need more hierarchy levels, you can cluster multiple sections into a section group. After you created a group, you can drag sections into the group. Another level you can create is Sub-pages. To be able to use them, you need to have at least two pages in a specific section.

For example, let's say you have a page with your meeting notes from Excel Conferences, you can create sub-pages with the notes for the individual sections. So you have a piece called Session Notes Excel Conference, and sub- pages for each section.

To create sub-pages, just click on the page you want to turn into a sub-page and select "Make subpage". It's going to indent the title. You can even have another level for sub-page that says sub-page of a sub-page. You don't have to use these as much, but if you have a lot of notes and need a detailed structure, they can be really helpful.

So to summarize, these are the different hierarchy levels, you can have: Notebook, section group, section, page, sub-page one, sub-page two. Just start with a structure that makes sense to you, you can always change it or add to it later.

The Interface

So, you have got Microsoft OneNote installed, what you have to do next is to click on the application and if you are starting this application for the first time you need to sign in with your Microsoft account, if you don't have one then you can click on "Create one" and it will take you to the Microsoft website where you can create your brand new account from Microsoft.

The beauty of this application is that whenever you log into your Microsoft OneNote it will automatically sync and download all the notes that you have created before, but if you are doing it for the first time then you won't see any notebook and you would have to create one.

The first thing that I want to introduce in OneNote is how it looks like. If you go up there in the left-hand corner, you have this thing that's called "Show Navigation". Go ahead and click on that, and that way you can organize your notes. The three main elements of OneNote are the Notebook, the Section, and the Page.

Pages are stored in sections, and sections are stored in notebooks. At the top here you can see the notebook account, then along the left-hand side, you can see the sections, which consists of Events, Meetings, Projects, Quick Notes, and Research.

If you click on the top bar, you will see all your notebooks. You could think of this as an actual physical notebook and you can have many different notebooks. If you want to create a new notebook, you come up to the notebook section at the top, and you can see your current notebook if you have any and also the option to look for more existing notebooks. Then you can come to the bottom and click on "Add new notebook" and that will give you the chance to give your notebook a title, after which you'll have a second notebook which you will see at the top.

To switch between notebooks, all you need to do is press on it, choose the other one and it will take you back to the other notebook.

Within a notebook, you could set up what are called Sections. Under the notebook, you have one section, and next to that you can see the pages within the sections.

If you want to create a new section within this notebook, you just go to the "Add section" button, give the section a title, and then you can add new pages to it by pressing "Add page". If you've already got a page when you press "Add page", it adds another and you just need to type the title in over on the right side to name it.

What you will do next is to rename the section as your Chapter One. Let's say this Unit has got two chapters, you can create one more section and give it the name of Chapter Two. What you may likely do next is to place these two chapters inside this Unit One; for that, you will simply drag it and drop it inside, so in this way, you can easily place these chapters inside this unit and if you click on the drop-down arrow under Unit One, then you can see how these chapters are hiding inside this subgroup section.

Not only can you create subgroups sections, but you can also create other groups as well. For that simply right-click and create a "New Section". Here you can see that you have created one Subgroup and inside that subgroup section you have added two sections, and then you have created the next Subgroup and inside it, you can have another section. So, whenever you want to move it, you can easily do that by dragging it upwards or downwards.

On each page, you can make a note. You can not only type there but you've got several options to draw, write or create handwritten notes and add images, links, and videos. We will look at these in detail in the next section.

Let's say you create a notebook to hold all your recipes. You can either right- click and select New Notebook, or you click on the Add notebook down here. The sections in this notebook could be the different types of dishes. So, you can create a section for appetizers, one for main dishes, one for vegetarian dishes, one for desserts, and so on. Within the sections, you add separate pages for the actual recipe. Using the example below, is a recipe for wild rice and mushroom burger. You can see that it has the ingredients, the directions, pictures, and even a link to where the recipe was gotten from.

Apart from recipes, you can have notebooks for ideas for videos with different sections depending on the progress, like brainstorming, research, or scripting. You can also have a notebook for private things like shopping lists, vacations and so on.

So you could organize your notebook as much or as little as you want but you have a lot of tools where you could set different hierarchies to your organization for OneNote, so quite a bit of power there.

Outstanding features in the different versions of OneNote This section summarizes the amazing features and benefits you can get with OneNote, giving you the specific versions where these features are available.

The feature of Copy Text from Pictures. This is only available in the version of OneNote that comes with Microsoft office. Remember that you can get this for free.

To copy text from pictures, well first off bring a picture into your OneNote file and when you click on the image you can extract the text by simply right-clicking on the image, and then there's an option you'll see that says "Copy Text from Picture". It's going to use OCR to extract all of the text from this image and you'll see all of the text from the image was extracted and pasted into the OneNote.

Microsoft OneNote makes it easy to consume content using the Immersive Reader. It improves the reading experience and then also you can have OneNote read to you. This is only available on the OneNote for the windows 10 app, and this is the app that comes pre-installed with Windows 10.

To use the immersive reader go up to the toolbar on top and select "View". Within the View ribbon, click on Immersive Reader and this opens up your text. First off, it removes all of the distractions around the text, increases the font size, and makes the spacings a lot better so it's easier to read the content. You can change my text preferences; highlight different parts of the speech and you can have OneNote help you focus on each line.

Another feature is the ability of OneNote to read to you. On the bottom of the Immersive reader, there is a play button, and next to that you'll see some voice settings, here you can set the voice speed and also choose whether it's a female or a male voice.

You can create Sticky Notes in the OneNote mobile app and have them automatically synchronize and show up on windows 10. First, you need to get the OneNote app. You can get that through the app store or the play store; it's free to download and install. Along with typing text, you can also insert a photo or change the color of the sticky note. On your Windows 10, go down to our taskbar, and type in sticky notes. This is an app that comes pre-installed and comes with windows 10, this launches the sticky notes app and you will see your note are in synchrony with that of your mobile app. This is a very nice way if you want to add sticky notes on the go and then get them onto your Windows 10 PC and vice versa. You can also add sticky notes on your Windows 10 PC and then they'll show up in your

OneNote app.

You can have Microsoft OneNote help you write meeting notes. This is handy if you've agreed to take notes for a meeting that's taking place. It is available in both versions of OneNote and you need to be using Microsoft Outlook to be able to take advantage of this. This inserts all of your meeting details; you can see the subject, date, location, and participants and once the meeting takes place you can start typing in your notes.

You can easily take tasks from your Microsoft OneNote and you could add it to your Microsoft to-do task list. Click over on the left of the text and there's your cursor, then go up to the Home tab, and over on the right-hand side there's an option for Outlook Tasks. When you click on that, it opens up a menu and you can now choose when the task is due. Once you pick your desired action, it adds a flag next to the item within your OneNote and this will now be synchronized over to Microsoft To-do and then also tasks within outlook. If you go to your Microsoft To-do task list, you'll see the task that you just added from OneNote. So, it synchronizes in both places and in your Microsoft Outlook, you will see that same task in your task list synchronized over from OneNote. This functionality is only available in the version of OneNote that comes with Microsoft office.

You could tag items in your OneNote to help you get back to them more easily in the future. This is available in all versions of OneNote. To make sure you remember something so could come back to it in the future, a tag can help you with that. Go to the Home tab and in the middle, you can see all the different tag options. You can even add your tags. Once you add the tag over on the left- hand side, you'll see that it added an important marker next to the item. If you want to get back to this tag in the future, right up above in the same area you can click on find tags. This now opens up a pane over on the right-hand side and there you see a summary of all of your important tags. So, this makes it easy to get back to the item. You can also see other tags that were used in the document and a category for tasks or dates those items are due.

Microsoft OneNote makes it very easy to collaborate with others. If you want to share a page with others, you can simply right-click on that and there's an option to copy a link to this page. Not only are you limited to copying pages, but you can also copy sections. Right at the top of a section, right-click, and here too you can copy a link to the entire section. Within outlook now you can simply go in and paste a link to the meeting notes and then other people can click on this and they'll be able to see your OneNote and then also work on your OneNote with you. This is available in both versions of OneNote.

You can easily password-protect a section of OneNote. This is available in both versions of OneNote. If you don't want anyone to be able to see a part of your section, when you right-click on the section you have the option to password- protect this section. While using this feature, please note that if you forget your password, you won't be able to get back your data so be very careful and make sure you remember your password.

You can easily convert handwriting into text that you can then edit on your computer. This works in both versions of the OneNote app. Doing this is extremely simple. Go up to the top toolbar, click on Draw, and over on the far right-hand side there's an option to turn Ink to Text. Clicking on that converts your hand-drawn text into editable text on your computer.

Did you know that you can set it so your OneNote window always appears as the topmost window especially when you're taking notes? You might have multiple windows open and your Note canvas within OneNote falls to the back. It would be nice to keep it always on top. Within OneNote click on the View tab and over on the far right-hand side of the ribbon there's the option to always keep OneNote on top. When you select this, you can click on your browser window or other content and your Note canvas will stay on top. This is only available in the OneNote app that comes with Microsoft office.

You can convert your OneNote into a full-screen mode to help you with note- taking. This is available in both versions. When you click on it, this gets rid of the ribbon and all the chrome of OneNote so you only see the canvas. Together with staying on top, this is a nice way to take notes on your PC.

You can easily translate text in OneNote and this is available in both versions of OneNote. To access "Translate", go to the bar on top, go over to Review and in the middle of the Review ribbon there is the option to translate. You could translate the selected text and you could open up a mini translator.

You can now choose what language it starts in and what language you want to translate to. After that, you have two options; you could insert it as is and this will replace the English text that I have over there, alternatively you can just copy it and paste it into your page.

To use the Mini Translator, within the Review ribbon click on "Translate" and then activate the Mini Translator. With the Mini Translator activated, when you hover over a word, you'll see a text box appear over there, and when you move your mouse over it, it'll show you the translation for this one specific word.

Did you know you could access previous versions of a OneNote page especially if you're storing your OneNote in OneDrive or SharePoint? This is available in both versions of the app. When you right-click on the translate option on a page where you have to translate, there at the bottom of the list there's the option to Show Page Versions. When you click on this you see a previous version of this page where you just had the English text and if you go to the current version, this version now has the translated text. As you work on a page over time, you'll see more versions stored.

If you start taking a lot of notes, sometimes it's nice to have multiple instances of OneNote open. If you currently have one copy of OneNote open and you want another one, it's easy to do that. Simply navigate down to your taskbar and right- click on the OneNote icon and then you can click on OneNote and this will open up another copy of OneNote. This too works with both versions of OneNote.

You can use OneNote to solve math equations. This is only available in OneNote for Windows 10. First, off you highlight the equation, next, you go up to the top toolbar and click on "Draw". Within the drawing ribbon, all the way over on the right-hand side click on the option that says "Math". When you click on Math, this shows you your equation over here, and below, you have a drop-down list where you can select an action. when you click on this you can solve the equation.

Another nice feature here is that there's another drop-down menu and when you click on that you can view the steps for solving the equation.

You can dictate to OneNote and it'll type up everything you say. Click on the Home tab and if you go to the right-hand side there's the option to "Dictate". Click on that and you can now start speaking. This is available in the OneNote for Windows 10 app.

CHAPTER 4: INPUT AND CUSTOMIZATION TECHNIQUES

Typing

To type on OneNote is the exact same process that you would do it on Word. You literally click anywhere and type. The key to these feature though is the use of the word 'anywhere.' Unlike word, where your typing is bound by invisible margins and rulers, in OneNote you can click and type anywhere on the page.

Doing this will create a small container that expands as you continue to type. The reason for this container is that once the note is written, you can pick it up and move it anywhere on the page – or to any section of the notebook, or any other notebook. For note taking purposes this means that you don't have to be aware of where the note it being written in comparison to others. It's once you have finished making the notes that you can move and pair them with similar ones.

Writing

If typing isn't your thing, OneNote allows for users to physically write and take notes by hand. Now, if you have a tablet that allows you use a pen on the screen, than all the better. If not than that's OK too.

A tab called 'draw,' is located at the top of the OneNote screen and in here you will find options for everything from line thickness to color. The real beauty of OneNote though comes in its ability to transcribe the drawing once you are done.

Pictures

Importing pictures into OneNote couldn't be simpler. In the

'Insert' tab you will see an 'Insert Picture,' option. Click this, open the relevant file and that's that. Just like with a container the picture can be picked up, moved and resized as you see fit.

One more cool function in regards to pictures. If there is a word in the picture, this word is actually searchable. So if you have saved a picture of a recipe for pie and later you search the word 'pie' than this recipe should come up.

Voice Records

Another great feature of OneNote is its ability to audio record. The process is rather simple too, all you need do is hit the 'Audio Recording' button, found in the 'Insert' tab, and it begins to record automatically.

This will then appear as an audio file in the relevant section and page.

There is one other great feature about this audio function that needs to be mentioned and that is that the audio is actually searchable. So let's say that the word 'dog,' is spoken and recorded. The user can then type the word 'dog,' into the search bar and the audio file will pop up.

Videos

OneNote is literally a do-all program. The team at Microsoft have made it there mission to make the gathering an organizing of notes as simple and effective as possible. No where else is this more evident than its ability to play video.

Say you find a great YouTube video that goes perfectly with the notes you are trying to make. All you need do it copy the page link to the video and paste it onto the page. It will then appear as a regular YouTube video that is watch-able on the page. You don't need to open the web browser again as OneNote does it all for you.

Tags

Tagging is a very important aspect of OneNote that should be utilized where possible. In the 'Home' tab you will see an entire section dedicated to tags. What these are little pictures that represent features of note taking. For example, a light-bulb represents an idea you might have for later, where a check mark represents something you need to do. All you need do is click and drag the tag to each relevant note in order to help it stand out more.

Another great feature, and a recent addition as of 2023, is the ability to search the tags. Next to the add tag location you will see a small icon labelled as 'Find Tags.' clicking on this will bring up a menu that lists all the tags you have used and where to find them.

Grids, Tables And Equations

Grids and tables can be made just like in a word document. And then it too can be picked up and moved. The unique thing about OneNote is that it then allows you to convert this table or gird into an excel spreadsheet. This will then allow you do use it in excel. From here you can convert the information into any number of graphs and charts as excel allows.

OneNote also has a very simple calculator function. Again, in the 'Insert tab,' you will see an option for 'equations.' This creates a small dialogue box for you to type simple equations into.

Webpages And Hyperlinks

First thing is first. hyperlinks can be copied and pasted into OneNote. It's simple and reasonably effective. But there is a better way to store the information see on a webpage for later use.

The first thing you will need to do this is download the add-on .Downloaded, this add-on should insert itself into your taskbar (this varies depending on the web browser that you are using).

Now, once you are on the page that you wish to add to OneNote, simply hit the clipper button. This will redirect you to a new menu which will give you the option of either inserting the whole page into OneNote, clipping just a fragment of the page yourself, or whether you want the clipper to do it for you. If for example you are clipping a page with a food recipe on it, the clipper function will convert the page so that only the recipe and photo of the food is showing.

The final product will then be downloaded to your default notebook and all you need do is move it to the relevant section and page.

Personalization

One final thing you are going to want to do is personalize your notebooks and sections. Again this is simple to do and usually done as a means to make your work more organized and accessible.

With OneNote you can personalize everything from the color of you notebook (this option is presented when you first create a new notebook) to the color of each section. You can also choose if you want each page to be lined, drawn up as a grid or just a blank page. And to take it even further, templates are available to add a flair to the background of each page too, such as flowers drawings and doodles.

OneNote is dedicated to making this working space as personalized and adaptable to your needs as possible.

CHAPTER 5: MASTERING SECTION GROUPS

Section groups are an attempt to implement the concept of a section and subsection. If you have a notebook for recipes and you're finding you have too many recipes for desserts (can one have too many dessert recipes?), you might want to reorganize your sections so you have a section for cakes and another section for pies and another section for ice cream, and then you can put all of those sections under a section group of desserts.

The problem with section groups is that they are implemented very oddly. On PC's and Mac's, section groups look very odd. On mobile devices, section groups look the way you might expect them to look, but there is only one very minor thing you can do with a section group on a mobile device. What Can You Do with a Section Group on a PC or Mac?

Create a New Section Group

Once you've selected your notebook, you're presented with a tabbed display of your sections. Right-click to the right of the tabs, and then click on New Section Group. This will create a section group aptly named New Section Group (with a number after it if you already happen to have a section group named New Section Group). The name of the section group is highlighted so if you just start typing, that will change the name of the section group.

You can also create a section group within a section group. Once you select your section group, you are presented with a tabbed display of your sections within that section group. If you then right-click to the right of the section tabs, you can create a new section group within this section group, just as you do within a notebook.

Select a Section Group

Once you've selected your notebook, click on the name of the section group (section groups are those multi-tabbed items to the right of the section tabs) you wish to select.

As a side note, section groups are always listed in alphabetical order, and you cannot change the order in which section groups are displayed.

As a further side note, if you attempt to change the order in which section groups are displayed by dragging and dropping a section group, you may well find that what you have really done is moved a section group to now be within another section group. Go ahead, ask how this was discovered.

Delete a Section Group

Right click on the section group you wish to delete, click on the Delete menu item, and then confirm you wish to move the section to Deleted Notes.

To see your Deleted Notes, click on the History menu, click on the down arrow associated with Notebook Recycle Bin, click on the Notebook Recycle Bin menu item, right-click the section you wish to restore, and then click on the Move or Copy menu item and tell OneNote where you wish to restore your deleted section.

WARNING: Deleted section groups are permanently deleted 60 days after you move the section group to the Deleted Notes.

Change the Name of a Section Group

Right-click the section group, click on the Rename menu item, and then type the new name into the tab.

Unlike with a section, you cannot double-click on a section group in order to rename a section group.

Move a Section Group

You can move a section group from one notebook to another notebook or to a section group. Right-click on the section group you wish to move, and then click on the Move... menu item. In the Move Section Group dialog, click on the notebook or section group to which you want to move this section group, and then click on the Move button.

Once the section group has been moved, the section group will now exist in the target notebook (and target section group, if you chose one), and the section group will no longer exist in its original location.

What Can You Do with a Section Group on a Mobile Device?

If you are viewing the sections within your selected notebook, you can see section groups with their sections under them. In the dessert example, above, you would see the Desserts section group with Cakes and Pies and Ice Cream listed as indented sections underneath Desserts.

Sync Section Group

On the page that lists your sections, long-press the desired section group, then press the "Sync section group" menu item.

While OneNote will automatically synchronize your notebooks, sections, and section groups in the background when it detects you've made changes, you can manually force the synchronization of a section group between your device and OneCloud to occur right now if you feel you need to do that for some reason.

CHAPTER 6: ENHANCING ONENOTE WITH ADD-INS

OneNote is a strong productivity tool on its own, but it has so much more potential if used with other third-party tools. Many of these are free, which make it even better to experiment.

The following tools are mainly focused on the desktop version, but some may also work on the mobile and web versions.

OneNote might not offer an "Insert" feature like many other note-taking programs, so to start using Add-ins you need to go to "File, Options, Add-ins" to add or remove each add-in.

Some downloads require a 32-bit or 64-bit version of OneNote. To find out which version of OneNote you have, go to "File, Account, About OneNote". The information should be displayed at the top of the page that pops up. This will help you to always download the right version of add-ins and prevent errors.

Here are some recommended Add-ins for you to try:

Learning Tools Add-in

This learning tool will help improve both your reading and writing skills. Whether you are a student, office worker, writer, or have dyslexia, this tool has all the features that may benefit you.

The tool includes many features, such as: Focus mode, Font spacing and short lines, Enhanced dictation, Immersive reading, Parts of speech, Syllabification, and Comprehension mode. For more detail, visit the official website: https://www.onenote.com/learningtools.

ONETASTIC and One Calendar Add-in

With ONETASTIC, you will be able to replicate some Word or Excel features in OneNote through the use of Macros. For example:

Tools such as Search and Replace, Table of Contents, Function, Favorites, Image Crop and Rotate, Custom Styles, Text select, etc.

There is a slight learning curve on macros, but there are tons of tutorials which will get you started, and definitely worth the effort.

ONETASTIC also give you access to One Calendar, a standalone tool that provides a calendar view.

Navigation in One Calendar is easy and has plenty of useful features. You can:

Switch to a different month/year, previous/next day, week, and month without having to toggle.

Customize your week to start on a Sunday or Monday.

Hovering over OneNote titles will give you a preview of the page. Search on the calendar.

View pages by the day it was created or modified. Display only the notebooks of your choice.

Click on the number of the day to get a view of the day. You can also switch between day, week, and month views by navigating to the button at the bottom right.

Customize it even further by using the Settings View, or Keyboard and mouse shortcuts.

Send to Sway Add-in

This tool will let you export data to Sway, which can then be used as a presentation in Microsoft PowerPoint or just to give your work some visual appeal. It allows you to present the information in fluid, dynamic ways. Sway is included in many Office 365 accounts, so if you have a subscription already, you can start using it immediately.

Class Notebook Add-in

Class Notebook is designed for teachers and other professionals to help manage work groups and classes more efficiently. The add-in creates an additional menu tab with all its new features. This includes:

Page and section distribution to a selected group of students.

Easy and fast review of work.

Assignment and grading integration with many Learning Management or Student Information systems.

Create assignments and set due dates. Post student's scores for an assignment.

Windows 10 and mac users don't have to download the add-in, as it is already built into OneNote.

There is also a OneNote Staff Notebook where teachers can share information and work together by planning lessons, taking notes, or discussing other developments.

OneNote Web Clipper

This is an extension for your web browser which allow you to capture information into your OneNote notebooks. It is different from the Send to OneNote add-in which is included with the desktop application. Sending to OneNote let you capture files on your desktop computer, Web Clipper record from the Internet, making research a faster and easier process.

Gem Add-in

This add-in combines over 400 features across 6 tabs to make OneNote more like other Office programs, or products such as Evernote. This includes table features, batch tools, reminders, anchor tools, batch tools, sorting, commonly used functions, etc.

Visit the official website for a list of all features: https://www.onenotegem.com/gem-for-onenote.html

Office Lens Add-in

Office Lens is available as a standalone app or built-in feature on Android or iOS devices. It allows you to take pictures of documents, business cards, or whiteboards, then enhances the photo to look like a scanned image much like the Evernote app does. The picture is then saved as a note and make the text on the image searchable.

OneNote Publisher for WordPress

If you are running a blog and do most of the work in OneNote, then OneNote Publisher for WordPress will come in handy. This tool lets you export your OneNote pages directly into your WordPress blog, thus eliminating the process of copy-and-pasting content yourself and re-doing all the formatting.

Customize the OneNote User Interface

The OneNote interface can be customized in many ways to enhance your experience with the program.

The desktop version let you change the default font for notes.

Having to change to your desired font or color each time you launch a note-taking program can grow tiresome, especially if you take notes a lot.

Like many other Microsoft programs, OneNote has several fonts pre-installed, but also allow you to add your own custom fonts.

To import a new font:

Download and unzip the specific font. Then simply search for Fonts in Control Panel, locate the file you have downloaded, and save it.

Not only can you change default fonts, but OneNote also allow you to adjust the default size of pages. This is a great way to make notes appear the same as they would on a smartphone or tablet, for example.

The option can be found on the View Tab under "Paper Size".

The desktop version also has a few themes and backgrounds for you to further customize the look and feel of the program.

This won't make any changes to pages and will have to be customized on their own. Page colors can be found on the View tab.

If you don't like the plain colors, add a background to a page by either adding a picture from the "Insert" tab or simply dragging and dropping the image into the page. Right-click on the inserted image to set it as a background.

Just like a paper notebook, sections can be categorized with different colors. Organizing sections by color will make your notes easier to find and also more attractive. Simply right-click on the section and choose "Section Color" to choose among 16 different colors.

If you are feeling overwhelmed by the number of tools shown on the screen or have no need for certain ones, then you can always choose which tools to display and also how you want them displayed by going to Options under the File Tab. For example, choose if you want Page or Navigation tabs to show on the left or right side of the interface.

Also customize the Ribbon area and Quick Access Toolbar by showing or hiding the tools of your choice to have a more organized and less cluttered appearance. Having control over the tools on the interface will help you take notes easier and make your work more efficient.

Example: If you use handwriting, stylus, or other drawing tools a lot, pin your preferred pen styles to the Quick Access Toolbar for easy access.

Also found in the Options menu: If English isn't your main language, you can change the default language to one you prefer. Depending on the language, you might need to download and install the additional language first.

OneNote pages has a wider width than other Office programs. If this bothers you, change the setting by using the "Fit Page Width to Window" setting in the View tab. To create a zoom effect, select the "Page Width" setting. This will match the page width to the window width.

OneNote has a Dock to Desktop feature which will dock the program to one side of your desktop. This is a very useful feature for easy access to your work if you are always making use of multiple programs. Either dock the whole application or several OneNote windows by choosing "Dock to Desktop" or New Docked Window" in the View tab.

Multitasking: Having the option to open more than one window make it easy to compare notes. But multiple open windows can also be annoying sometimes if the smaller windows keep disappearing behind the larger ones. Luckily OneNote has an "Always on Top" feature in the View tab which will always focus the selected window.

Rule and Grid lines: OneNote pages are a white blank by default. If you need to fit images or other objects a certain way and need lines to guide you, there are a few different rule or grid lines to enable under the View tab. You can also customize them by changing the color. Just note that the lines won't show up on printouts, so use them only to plan drafts.

Remove titles, time, and date: If you don't want to see the title of a note, or the displayed time and date, remove it by clicking on the "Hide Note Title" in the View tab. Be aware that this option completely removes it and not just hide from view.

For people who want to access notes even faster to save time and be more productive: use shortcuts, widgets, or live tiles. On your smartphone, for example, you can either set a shortcut on the home screen or make use of the very useful screen widget to make quick notes. If you are using windows 8 and up, set live tiles on the start menu or pin to taskbar.

CHAPTER 7: ONENOTE FOR EFFECTIVE PROJECT MANAGEMENT

After having spent more than 15 years in IT project management, I appreciate the tools that make project management easier and more efficient. OneNote (yes, OneNote!) Is such a tool. Today I want to emphasize how a project manager and members of the project team can utilize and receive OneNote when overseeing ventures inside an association.

It is imperative to take note of that OneNote is not a project management software in itself. However, OneNote, in combination with SharePoint Site or Office 365 Group or Planner - does this. So when I talk about the features of OneNote below, the software is more of a help/facilitation tool that complements the other tools in the Office 365 ecosystem.

Storing And Sharing Of Agendas

OneNote can be ideal for storing calendars for gatherings. You can make a page for each gathering and give it a name accordingly.

Because OneNote is standard on all SharePoint sites and Office 365 groups, you can use it to collaborate and create together and easily ask your team members by adding items to a calendar. for example.

Keep The Minutes Of The Meeting

Another great piece of content owned by OneNote is minutes. You can utilize the equivalent OneNote page where you have saved the above agenda items and save meeting notes, actions, and other meeting results so that everything stays in one place. You can also create another meeting minute page and organize it with the calendar page above in a section.

If you manage your projects using the Agile method, OneNote can become a great tool to keep track of these daily Scrum meetings. I have documented it in this message.

Save The Lessons Learned

Another incredible method to utilize OneNote is to catch exercises learned about a project. When I led projects in the business world, I held lessons for lessons learned for each project I managed. This helped me prevent errors in future projects.

And then you can allow users to write together and contribute to the document, essentially by creating a database of lessons learned.

Organization Of Risks In A Risk Register

Another interesting way to use OneNote is to record project risks. In general, the risk register is built in Excel, I also recommend using a custom SharePoint list for this, list for this, yet you can likewise utilize OneNote and embed an Excel table or document directly on the page.

Wiki Project

What makes OneNote great - is that it can become an easy dump (repository) for all content (images, audio, video, tables, handwritten notes, etc.) that would otherwise not be stored in a SharePoint document library. You can use the sections and pages of OneNote to create a fun Wiki project! OneNote is completely accessible, so you can generally find and find what you are looking for.

Status Reports

Oh yes, situation reports! Who doesn't love them? Well, the truth is that nobody does it except senior management. I remember that when managing projects in the business world, I disliked having them in the same place. You dedicate a lot of time to a thing that would take senior managers 1 minute to read, only to make a stupid and unreasonable decision. Sorry, I wandered here. Either way, OneNote tends towards being an incredible tool to accelerate the development of these weekly status reports.

List Of Methods

Action Items is one of the many contents that could be perfect for OneNote. This can be ideal for quick task lists that are not part of the formal task list/planning.

The checklist (To-Do functionality in OneNote) is great!

E-Mails

Have you received an important e-mail in which you are invited to be part of a project file? With one click on the button, you can copy the entire e-mail to every OneNote notebook.

How One Note Is Efficiently Use By Project Calendar And Insurance Organizing OneNote is a fantastic Microsoft program that often goes unnoticed and is underused. It is a great productivity tool because it focuses on taking notes, both typed and handwritten, audio recording, search tools and has great integration with the rest of Microsoft Office programs. Until recently, I was still in the old school and I wrote all my notes in a spiral-bound notebook, but I discovered OneNote. It is as if you have a digital notebook that organizes pages for you and makes sharing information with your colleagues much easier and does the job much more efficiently. Below you will find only a handful of options that OneNote has to offer to make your experience taking notes even better.

What Makes OneNote Special? Trusted Interface

OneNote uses a trusted interface that is already part of other MS Office tools, such as Word, Excel, PowerPoint. It has a horizontal ribbon on the top, where you can access all the usual commands and operations.

Logical Hierarchy

OneNote follows a "paper" notebook approach to organize and store notes electronically. Just like with the traditional paper notebook, where you have different pages and sections, OneNote follows the same terminology and methodology. In OneNote, you can create the following:

Pages

The pages are your usual pages in a notebook. For example, you can create a page for each meeting where the meeting agenda and minutes are saved.

Sections

The pages are then organized into sections. The part is how you usually split your paper notebook, right? So you can have a part for meetings, apart from project problems, business requirements, etc.

Integration With Outlook

OneNote has really cool coordination with Outlook. You can extract the meeting details in OneNote from Outlook. Similarly, you can include notes in your appointment invitation by simply clicking a button. No more attachments and users ask them to send a plan!

Mobile-Friendly

Much the same as SharePoint, OneDrive and different MS Office instruments, OneNote additionally has a portable application. This makes OneNote effectively available from the "field," where there is no opportunity to make formal records.

Online Edition

Just like the rest of the MS Office tools, OneNote can be edited in the browser. This indicates that there is no need whatsoever to download the file or even install OneNote if you want to make changes to OneNote quickly 'on the fly.'

See Microsoft OneNote As A Digital Version Of A Physical Laptop.

This means that you can take digital notes and keep them organized. It also means that you can add images, diagrams, sound, video, etc. Use OneNote with other Office package programs, on your desktop or your mobile devices.

With these simple steps, you can get started quickly, even if you are a complete beginner. Then we will link you to more intermediate and advanced tips to ensure that you get the most out of this useful program.

Useful tips and tricks for Microsoft OneNote Extract text from images

Unknown to most and easy to learn, with this feature, you can create an image with a recognizable font and copy the text to your page. Perfect for screenshots and extensive images, this handy item can save you from retyping sentences or even paragraphs. Here's how you can extract text from images in Microsoft OneNote.

Search in all your notes

OneNote is a great organizational tool, but sometimes things can get lost. Instead of clicking on all your sections and pages, search your notes to find that missing item.

Integrate OneNote with Outlook tasks

If you want to control online ordering, this tip is for you. Synchronize your Microsoft OneNote task list with your Outlook e-mail and ensure that all tasks are before you. Avoid the hassle of switching windows and learn how to integrate Microsoft OneNote tasks with Microsoft Outlook.

Perform simple calculations without a calculator

The ability to make calculations without a calculator or preprogrammed formula is smart and useful. By applying the simplest mathematical functions, you can perform calculations on the spot. So don't take your calculator out of your house, let OneNote take care of your computing needs. You can perform calculations without a calculator in Microsoft OneNote as follows.

Make a digital note

If you are busy at work and have a random thought to be noted, Microsoft OneNote is there for you. Clicking on WINDOWS + N opens a digital note on your computer. With this note, you can type, draw, insert attachments or record audio. Simply close and the note will be saved in your quick notes. Here you will find more information about digital sticky notes.

Integrate documents and spreadsheets into your notes

Constantly switching between Windows on your computer can be annoying. Fortunately, Microsoft OneNote has a solution: you can integrate any saved document or spreadsheet into your notes. The inserted file is then treated as an image so that you can only refer to the content and cannot change it. You can embed documents and spreadsheets in your notes in Microsoft OneNote as follows.

Work together via Microsoft OneNote

If you want someone else to view parts of your OneNote notebook, share it with him. Sharing your notes makes collaboration easier because you and your colleagues can man oeuvre through organized plans and ideas. You can share your notes in Microsoft OneNote as follows.

Microsoft OneNote is a great tool to use. By using the many possibilities, your organizational skills will certainly improve considerably. Therefore, apply these seven tips and tricks from Microsoft OneNote to get the most out of this practical and flexible software.

How Organizations Use OneNote

The great thing about OneNote is that due to its nature (informal notes) it can be used in different ways. Here are some examples I have seen from my experience:

Project meeting artefacts

OneNote is ideal for project management. I even blogged about OneNote that is widely used in the field of project management. You can use the OneNote pages to communicate meeting calendars, meeting minutes, and project status.

User comments / informal requirements / wish lists

OneNote can also be a great tool for collecting, for example, a business requirement for software or user wish list/feedback items. Until you have an official document, OneNote can also become a "dump" for users to enter and type what they want. This can be a quick way to collect user feedback without having to set up complex surveys or structure.

CHAPTER 8: EVALUATING ONENOTE'S EFFECTIVENESS

Applications like OneNote are created and features are added taking into account the evolving needs of the user. It is, thus fair to say that such applications, including OneNote, are not exactly perfect. While this application is designed to offer users a wide array of features that they look for, it is important that they are aware of its limitations so they know what to expect. Here are the pros and cons of OneNote applications:

Pros

The Stack Interface: Whether you have been using OneNote for a long time or you are just getting started, you can tell that the interface makes the whole application user-friendly. No matter what platform you run the app on, you can be assured that it will be easy to figure out.

Color Divider: If you want everything color coded, OneNote app is able to do this and enhance your ability to keep things organized. The app also enables you to organize individual tabs using color codes so they are easy to find based on their colors.

Easy to Run on All Devices: If you have a Windows powered laptop, or even a Mac powered one, you can run the OneNote app. The app also runs on all phone platforms are available in the market. Though the features may differ a bit depending on the platform designs, most tend to be more compatible with Windows version of OneNote. However, the app can generally run on any platform.

Elegant Look: Everyone wants to use an application that looks good. OneNote comes with a simple but elegant look that appeals to most users.

Easy to Integrate with Other Documents: If you want to place a portion of content from Word files to notebooks that you have created, or vice versa, OneNote allows you to do this with relative ease. The latest versions of OneNote are integrated with MS Word and Excel, an aspect that allows users to add Excel files to OneNote and review them from the app.

Cons

Newbies May Find OneNote Hard to Understand in the Beginning: New users are likely to find OneNote tricky to understand. This is especially true for the Windows version that comes with a wide variety of improved features. It might be a bit complicated in the beginning, but after spending time interacting with the application, one becomes accustomed to it and finds it easier to use.

The Application is not the same for all platforms:

OneNote does not use the same design across all operating systems and phone platforms. The features vary from one platform to another. Each operating system has its own design, an aspect that presents a challenge to people who want to use it on different platforms. On the Windows operating system, users are able to do more with OneNote compared to Mac or iOS platforms. For instance, the Mac version is less than stellar because of the limited features available.

Mac Users cannot Embed Videos: While it is possible to add files, text and other details on notes created on OneNote, users cannot add videos to the Mac version of this application. This feature is only available in the Windows version of OneNote.

Comparison of OneNote with Other Applications
Comparison of One Note with Evernote

The release of OneNote was direct competition for another application referred to as EverNote, is interesting considering how popular EverNote has been.

EverNote has dominated the market for a very long time, but it was about time to release a program that will cover up some of the shortcomings of EverNote. The two programs have been designed to work on the same platforms but they have very distinctive features, which makes OneNote much better than the popular EverNote in one sense and EverNote better than OneNote in the other sense.

OneNote is a great way to get organized, something that EverNote does not offer to its users. With OneNote, you can create simple to complex notes from the beginning, organize them into notebooks that can be searched and browsed and even make them accessible through different platforms through synchronization. You can easily access your notes, plus all their details from OneNote with little or no effort.

OneNote's note creation tools are much more advanced than those of EverNote. If you are the kind of user that needs software that will create great quality notes and help you organize them, you will be much better using OneNote. However, it is incapable of clipping notes from the internet like EverNote and this is its main shortcoming.

OneNote gives its users access to many different kinds of features and this means that it is much more useful than its counterpart. If you are looking for software that will give you more benefits between the two, it is best to go for OneNote but always remember that there are features from EverNote that you may not get from OneNote.

However, if you are looking for software that will also allow you to find, capture and organize content from the internet, OneNote will not be great for this, but

EverNote.

Both EverNote and OneNote is note taking tools but their features make them so different in what they offer to their clients. You will choose what to go for depending on what you want to achieve. The good thing is that you can always use both of them for their different features so as to ensure that you are achieving more every day and making things easier for yourself.

Why OneNote is better than EverNote?

OneNote and EverNote are two applications that compete to become market leaders in the note taking space. These two notetaking applications tend to be compared to each other often because they tend to appeal to various users and each has features that gives it an edge. Most importantly, there are functions that OneNote can perform that EverNote currently cannot.

Such functions include adding text to files, adding images and doodling and writing ideas that come to mind. A lot of the functionality in OneNote depends on a user's ability to personalize it, which makes it better than EverNote. Here are details of what a user can do using OneNote, differently than when he uses EverNote.

Integrating Office

Unlike EverNote, integration with Office is possible with OneNote. This is perhaps the case because EverNote is not connected to other software like OneNote is to Office. With the former, users cannot include Word documents but this is easy to do with OneNote. Adding Videos to Notes When using the OneNote for Windows, one can take notes in a different way compared to how they take down notes using traditional methods, Instead of drawing comic strips to keep things interesting, you can easily add videos to your notes and make things work well for you. This is not the case with the EverNote app.

Keep To Do Lists Organized

You can expect that aside from your OneNote notebook, there is a lot more to do with the app like ensuring lists are organized. This is easily achieved by adding tabs to pages of a notebook. Users can also compare their lists using sticky notes if they so wish. On OneNote, sticky notes may be placed just like they are added on a typical notebook.

Get Additional Storage for Free

For those who take notes on different things and need plenty of space, OneNote comes in handy. The app offers users free storage space of up to 15 GB with ease. This amount of space is not bad at all when you think of how much text and images you need to generate to fill it up.

From the things mentioned above, it is evident that OneNote offers a lot of things that EverNote app cannot.

Comparison of OneNote with Google Keep

While people never thought that Google Keep will be revived by Google again, the app was coming back to the market to compete with EverNoteas well as OneNote. The Google Keep app is available to users for free when used online as well as for download on Android powered devices.

On the other hand, OneNote is part of the Microsoft Office 365 subscription. It can come as part of the package when purchased alongside other applications that are useful in devices. Like Google Keep, OneNote is can be used for free online. A free version of the app is also available for users who do not wish to spend money on it. The OneNote Office version is considered better compared to other versions because it has the ability to take screenshots that can be printed out directly.

So far, Google Keep does not have applications that can be used on Android and iOS devices. What this means is that users can only access and use it online with either a laptop or desktop computer. Eventually, Google might release something similar to what OneNote is already offering to the general public, but for now, it is evident that OneNote is the perfect choice for people looking for an efficient note-taking application.

When it comes to text editing, it is easy to tell that OneNote app is superior mainly because of the rich text formatting features that come with it. These features allow users to organize the text they place on their notebooks appropriately. With Google Keep, it is not possible to do this. Instead of organizing text, pressing the enter button creates a new file on Google Keep

Google Keep tends to be a choice for people who want to keep things simple. However, if you are not just looking at simplicity, but want to experience a wide range of ways to get things done completed while exploring different features that enhance your ability to keep notes intact, OneNote is your best choice.

Other Applications Similar to OneNote

EverNote and Google Keep are two among other applications that are considered to be very similar to OneNote. However, but there are others that offer similar features. They include the following:

CintaNotes: Just as its name suggests this is an application that allows you to add notes is a very straightforward way. Though this application is pretty simple and easy to use, it does not come with most features that OneNote offers. Compared to OneNote, its features are very basic and limited.

NeverNote: This was initially created to run on Linux operating system and is only after some time that it became available for Windows platforms. While NeverNote serves more as a response to EverNote than OneNote, it is not very functional.

TiddlyWiki: If you have been looking for apps to enable you organize your documents better, you may have come across this application before finding. While it does much of what OneNote can do, OneNote can still do that those things much better. There are many shortcuts that one has to learn before they can use the TiddlyWiki application with ease compared to OneNote. OneNote does not require users to learn numerous shortcuts to use it, an aspect that makes it distinct from TiddlyWiki

It is clear that there are different applications and software available for note taking running on various platforms. When you compare all these applications, OneNote still emerges as the best choice. This is largely due to the options in terms of features that it offers users that build their confidence in organizing their personal and work related things based on their needs.

CHAPTER 9: KEYBOARD SHORTCUTS IN ONENOTE

Frequently used shortcuts

To do this	Press
Open a new OneNote window.	Ctrl+M
Create a **Quick Note**.	Ctrl+Shift+M or Alt+Windows logo key+N
Dock the OneNote window.	Ctrl+Alt+D
Undo the previous action.	Ctrl+Z
Redo the previous action, if possible.	Ctrl+Y
Select all items on the current page.	Ctrl+A To expand the selection, press Ctrl+A again.
Cut the selected text or item.	Ctrl+X
Copy the selected text or item to the clipboard.	Ctrl+C
Paste the contents of the clipboard.	Ctrl+V
Move to the beginning of the line.	Home
Move to the end of the line.	End
Move one word to the left.	Ctrl+Left arrow key

To do this	Press
Move one word to the right.	Ctrl+Right arrow key
Delete one character to the left.	Backspace
Delete one character to the right.	Delete
Delete one word to the left.	Ctrl+Backspace
Delete one word to the right.	Ctrl+Delete
Insert a line break without starting a new paragraph.	Shift+Enter
Check spelling.	F7
Open the thesaurus for the currently selected word.	Shift+F7
Display the context menu for the currently focused object.	Shift+F10 or Windows Menu key
Perform the action suggested on the **Information Bar** when it appears at the top of a page.	Ctrl+Shift+W
Play the selected audio recording.	Ctrl+Alt+P
Stop audio recording playback.	Ctrl+Alt+S
Skip the current audio recording backward by 10 seconds.	Ctrl+Alt+Y
Skip the current audio recording forward by 10 seconds.	Ctrl+Alt+U

Format notes

To do this	Press
Highlight the selected text.	Ctrl+Alt+H
Insert a hyperlink.	Ctrl+K
Copy the formatting of the selected text (**Format Painter**).	Ctrl+Shift+C
Paste the formatting to the selected text (**Format Painter**).	Ctrl+Shift+V
Open a hyperlink.	Enter when on the hyperlink text
Apply or remove bold formatting.	Ctrl+B
Apply or remove italics formatting.	Ctrl+I
Apply or remove underline formatting.	Ctrl+U
Apply or remove strikethrough formatting.	Ctrl+Hyphen (-)
Apply or remove superscript formatting.	Ctrl+Shift+Equal sign (=)
Apply or remove subscript formatting.	Ctrl+Equal sign (=)
Apply or remove bulleted list formatting.	Ctrl+Period (.)
Apply or remove numbered list formatting.	Ctrl+Forward slash (/)
Apply a **Heading 1** style to the current note.	Ctrl+Alt+1
Apply a **Heading 2** style to the current note.	Ctrl+Alt+2

To do this	Press
Apply a **Heading 3** style to the current note.	Ctrl+Alt+3
Apply a **Heading 4** style to the current note.	Ctrl+Alt+4
Apply a **Heading 5** style to the current note.	Ctrl+Alt+5
Apply a **Heading 6** style to the current note.	Ctrl+Alt+6
Clear all formatting applied to the selected text. (Apply the **Normal** style.)	Ctrl+Shift+N
Increase the paragraph indent.	Alt+Shift+Right arrow key or the Tab key when at the beginning of a line
Decrease the paragraph indent.	Alt+Shift+Left arrow key or Shift+Tab when at the beginning of a line
Align the paragraph to the left.	Ctrl+L
Align the paragraph to the right.	Ctrl+R
Increase the font size of the selected text.	Ctrl+Shift+Right angle bracket (>)
Decrease the font size of the selected text.	Ctrl+Shift+Left angle bracket (<)

To do this	Press
Show or hide the rule lines on the current page.	Ctrl+Shift+R

Insert items on a page

To do this	Press
Insert a document or file on the current page.	Alt+N, F
Insert a document or file as a printout on the current page.	Alt+N, O
Show or hide document printouts on the current page when the high contrast mode on Windows 10 or one of the contrast themes on Windows 11 is activated.	Alt+Shift+P
Insert a picture from a file.	Alt+N, P
Insert a sticker.	Alt+N, S
Insert a screen clipping. **Note:** The OneNote icon must be active in the Windows taskbar notification area.	Windows logo key+Shift+S, and then Ctrl+V In OneNote 2007 and 2010, Windows logo key+S
Insert the current date.	Alt+Shift+D
Insert the current date and time.	Alt+Shift+F
Insert the current time.	Alt+Shift+T
Insert a line break.	Shift+Enter

To do this	Press
Start a math equation or convert selected text to a math equation.	Alt+Equal sign (=)

Work with tables

To do this	Press
Create a table.	Tab key after typing a new line of text
Create another column in a table with a single row.	Tab key
Create another row when at the end cell of a table.	Enter **Note:** Press Enter again to finish creating the table.
Insert a row below the current row.	Ctrl+Enter when in a table cell
Create another paragraph in the same cell in a table.	Alt+Enter
Create a column to the right of the current column in a table.	Ctrl+Alt+R
Create a column to the left of the current column in a table.	In OneNote 2010, Ctrl+Alt+E
Create a row above the current one in a table.	Enter when the cursor is at the beginning of any row, except for the first row

To do this	Press
Create a new cell or row.	Tab key when in the last cell of the table
Delete the current empty row in a table.	Delete, then Delete again, when the cursor is at the beginning of the row

Select text and objects

To do this	Press
Select all items on the current page.	Ctrl+A To expand the selection, press Ctrl+A again.
Select to the end of the line from the current cursor location.	Shift+End
Select the whole line.	Shift+Down arrow key when the cursor is at the beginning of the line
Jump to the title of the page and select it.	Ctrl+Shift+T
Cancel selecting the outline or page.	Esc
Move the selected paragraphs upward.	Alt+Shift+Up arrow key

To do this	Press
Move the selected paragraphs downward.	Alt+Shift+Down arrow key
Increase the paragraph indent.	Alt+Shift+Left arrow key
Decrease the paragraph indent.	Alt+Shift+Right arrow key
Select the current paragraph and its subordinate paragraphs.	Ctrl+Shift+Hyphen (-)
Delete the selected note or object.	Delete
Move to the beginning of the line.	Home
Move to the end of the line.	End
Go back to the last page visited.	Alt+Left arrow key
Go forward to the next page visited.	Alt+Right arrow key

CONCLUSION

As we reach the conclusion of this journey through the Microsoft OneNote Quick Start 2024 Guide, it's time to reflect on the vast landscape we have traversed. From the initial introduction to OneNote's interface to mastering advanced features, this guide has aimed to transform your understanding and use of this powerful tool.

Recapitulating the Journey

We began with the basics, understanding the layout and the primary functions of OneNote. This foundation was crucial for what was to come, as OneNote is more than just a note-taking application; it's a comprehensive platform for organizing, managing, and sharing information. The chapters gradually built upon this foundation, introducing more sophisticated features and techniques.

Key Features and Advancements

Throughout the guide, we highlighted the key features and advancements in the 2024 edition of OneNote. These enhancements, from improved integration with other Microsoft 365 tools to advanced collaboration capabilities, mark a significant step forward in digital organization tools. We delved into practical applications, showing how these features could be leveraged in various scenarios, from business and education to personal projects.

Customization and Flexibility

One of the central themes of this guide has been the incredible customization and flexibility that OneNote offers. Whether it was through setting up tailored notebooks, utilizing tags for efficient information retrieval, or integrating with other applications for a seamless digital experience, the versatility of OneNote stood out. This guide provided the knowledge to mold OneNote according to your unique needs and workflows.

Collaboration and Sharing

In a world where collaboration is key, we explored how OneNote excels in enabling teamwork and information sharing. The guide illustrated how shared notebooks and real-time editing can revolutionize group projects and remote work. The importance of OneNote in a post-pandemic world, where remote and hybrid work models have gained prominence, was particularly emphasized.

Beyond Note-Taking: A Tool for Life

OneNote is not just a tool for note-taking; it's a companion for life's various endeavors. Throughout the guide, we saw its application in diverse contexts - from managing complex projects to simple daily tasks. The aim was to show that OneNote could adapt to any requirement, making it an indispensable tool in your digital arsenal.

Preparing for the Future

As technology continues to evolve, so will OneNote. This guide has equipped you with the skills and knowledge to not only use OneNote effectively today but to adapt to future updates and changes. The journey with OneNote doesn't end here; it evolves as you continue to explore and utilize its capabilities.

Harnessing OneNote for Personal and Professional Growth

As you integrate OneNote into your daily routine, you'll find it's more than a tool; it's a catalyst for personal and professional growth. The skills and techniques outlined in this guide encourage a more organized, efficient approach to managing information. Whether it's keeping track of important family events, managing a complex business project, or organizing research for academic purposes, OneNote's versatility shines through. This guide aimed to empower you to harness this potential to its fullest.

Embracing a Digital-First Approach

The 2024 edition of OneNote represents a broader shift towards a digital-first approach in our work and personal lives. By embracing this shift and utilizing OneNote, you're not just staying current with technological trends; you're positioning yourself at the forefront of digital productivity. This guide has shown how OneNote can be a central part of this transformation, offering solutions that are both innovative and intuitive.

The Evolution of Collaboration

OneNote's capabilities in fostering collaboration cannot be overstated. As the world becomes increasingly interconnected, the ability to work together effectively, regardless of physical location, becomes crucial. This guide illustrated how OneNote's collaborative features can bridge distances, creating a cohesive environment for sharing ideas and knowledge. The importance of this in a world that values connectivity and collaborative intelligence cannot be understated.

Personalizing Your OneNote Experience

Personalization has been a recurring theme in this guide. OneNote's true power lies in its ability to be tailored to your individual needs. Throughout the chapters, we provided insights on customizing OneNote, from creating personalized templates to setting up specific workflows. This personalization extends to accessibility as well, ensuring that OneNote is usable and helpful to as wide an audience as possible.

Looking Ahead: OneNote and the Future

As we conclude, it's important to look ahead. The technology landscape is constantly evolving, and with it, so will OneNote. This guide has laid a foundation, but your journey with OneNote is just beginning. Staying abreast of updates and continuously exploring OneNote's capabilities will ensure that you remain at the cutting edge of digital organization and productivity.

Final Reflections

In closing, the "Microsoft OneNote Quick Start 2024 Guide" was more than a manual; it was a journey through the possibilities of digital organization and collaboration. OneNote is a tool that grows with you, adapting to your changing needs and the evolving digital landscape. As you move forward, carry the insights and knowledge from this guide, and let OneNote be a partner in your journey towards greater efficiency, organization, and collaboration.

Remember, the true potential of OneNote lies in how you choose to use it. Whether you're a student, a professional, or someone simply looking to bring more order to your digital life, OneNote offers a universe of possibilities. Explore, experiment, and experience how this powerful tool can transform your approach to information management and collaboration.

Final Thoughts

In conclusion, Microsoft OneNote is more than just an application; it's a gateway to enhanced productivity, organization, and collaboration. This guide aimed to demystify OneNote, making it accessible and useful for all. As you close this book, remember that the journey with OneNote is ongoing. The more you use it, the more you will discover its potential to transform your digital life.

Printed in Great Britain
by Amazon